$6.99
AZ/HS

Fever 17

by
Laurie Halse Anderson

Student Packet

Written by
Betsy McCorry

Contains masters for:
2 Prereading Activities
8 Vocabulary Activities
1 Study Guide
1 Comprehension Activity
1 Literary Analysis Activity
2 Character Analysis Activities
2 Critical Thinking Activities
1 Writing Activity
4 Quizzes
Novel Test
PLUS Detailed Answer Key
and Scoring Rubric

Note

The Aladdin Paperbacks edition of the book, © 2002, was used to prepare this guide. The page references may differ in other editions. Novel ISBN: 0-689-84891-9

Please note: Parts of this novel deal with sensitive, mature issues. Please assess the appropriateness of this book for the age level and maturity of your students prior to reading and discussing it with them.

ISBN 1-58130-895-7

Printed in the United States of America.

To order, contact your local school supply store, or—

Novel Units, Inc.
P.O. Box 97
Bulverde, TX 78163-0097

Web site: www.educyberstor.com

Name ________________________________

Clue Search

Directions: Collect information about the book for each of the items. Write down the information and then make some predictions about the book.

Information Source	Information Provided
Dedication	
Title	
Cover Illustration	
Teasers on the cover	
Friends' recommendations	
Reviewers' recommendations/awards won	

Your predictions about the book:

Name ______________________________

Directions: Match the terms in Column A to the correct description in Column B.

Column A	Column B
____ 1. George Washington	a. third President of the United States
____ 2. New York City; Philadelphia; Washington, D.C.	b. 1783
____ 3. The Revolutionary War ends.	c. United States capitals
____ 4. Thomas Jefferson	d. 1788
____ 5. City of Brotherly Love	e. 1865
____ 6. The Declaration of Independence is signed.	f. 1776
____ 7. The United States Constitution is ratified (adopted).	g. Philadelphia
____ 8. Slavery is abolished.	h. first President of the United States

Name ______________________________

Vocabulary Sentence Sets

wretched (2)	abhorred (3)	dawdling (3)	corpse (4)
musket (10)	disreputable (11)	robust (15)	peculiar (15)
noxious (20)	interjected (20)	colleague (20)	exhausted (22)

Directions: Write the vocabulary words on the numbered lines below.

1. ______________________________ 2. ______________________________
3. ______________________________ 4. ______________________________
5. ______________________________ 6. ______________________________
7. ______________________________ 8. ______________________________
9. ______________________________ 10. ______________________________
11. ______________________________ 12. ______________________________

On a separate sheet of paper, use each of the following sets of words in an original sentence. Your sentences should show that you know the meanings of the vocabulary words as they are used in the story.

Sentence 1: words 8 and 4
Sentence 2: words 9 and 3
Sentence 3: words 1 and 10
Sentence 4: words 11 and 7
Sentence 5: words 3 and 6
Sentence 6: words 12 and 4
Sentence 7: words 8 and 9
Sentence 8: words 5 and 2
Sentence 9: words 7 and 6

Fever 1793
Activity #4 • Vocabulary
Chapters Five–Seven, pp. 24–53

Name ______________________________

Vocabulary Wheel

accommodate (26)	solemnly (28)	drought (29)	impudence (31)
tolled (32)	absentmindedly (34)	condolences (35)	busybodies (35)
droll (37)	overwhelming (44)	hilarious (49)	dilemma (49)
tedious (50)			

Directions: Write each vocabulary word on a piece of paper (one word per piece). Make a spinner using the circle below. Now play the following game with a classmate. (It is a good idea to have a dictionary and thesaurus handy.) Place the papers in a small container. The first player draws a word from the container. The player then spins the spinner and follows the direction where the pointer lands. For example, if the player draws the word "droll" and lands on "define," the player must define the word droll. If the player's partner accepts the answer as correct, the first player scores one point and play passes to the second player. If the player's partner challenges the answer, the first player uses a dictionary or thesaurus to prove the answer is correct. If the player can prove the answer is correct, the player earns two points. If the player cannot prove the answer is correct, the opposing player earns two points. Play continues until all the words have been used. The player with the most points wins.

Name ______________________________

Vocabulary Word Map

purify (54)	din (54)	gumption (56)	apprentice (57)
pondered (59)	straddle (60)	respite (60)	pestilence (60)
vehemently (61)	quarrelsome (64)	fractious (64)	recoiled (69)
imposter (71)	peril (73)	bellowed (76)	hoisting (77)

Directions: Choose five vocabulary words from the list above and complete a word map for each word.

Synonyms

____

____

____

Antonyms

____

____

____

WORD

____

Definition in your own words

____

____

____

Used in a sentence

____

____

____

Name ______________________________

contracted (82)	haste (83)	canteen (85)	cherub (86)
pursuit (87)	mantle (87)	skirmish (87)	prying (90)
raspy (92)	embers (93)	gnarled (94)	slovenly (102)
destitute (106)	famished (107)		

Directions: Choose the BEST answer to replace the underlined word.

1. My brother contracted the flu after visiting his sick friend.
   a. caught
   b. inhaled
   c. achieved

2. Our teacher told us to take our time and not make haste when we practice our handwriting.
   a. waste time
   b. hurry
   c. criticize

3. The soldier took a drink of water from his canteen.
   a. glass
   b. thermos
   c. pitcher

4. My grandmother says that I'm her little cherub.
   a. angel
   b. monster
   c. daughter

5. The police were in pursuit of the escaped prisoner.
   a. fear
   b. chase
   c. surprise

6. Her tunic served as a mantle for her bathing suit.
   a. accessory
   b. cover
   c. replacement

7. When the principal saw the skirmish on the playground, he made the children separate and sit by the wall until recess was over.
   a. game
   b. party
   c. fight

Name ________________________________

8. Mother told me to stop <u>prying</u> into other people's business.
   a. snooping
   b. jumping
   c. ignoring

9. He had a sore throat, so he spoke with a very <u>raspy</u> voice.
   a. soft
   b. scratchy
   c. noiseless

10. Long after the fire went out, there were still <u>embers</u> in the fireplace.
    a. live coals
    b. sticks
    c. flames

11. The roots of the old tree were <u>gnarled</u>.
    a. black
    b. knotty
    c. split

12. Since their mother was out of town and their cousin was taking care of them, the children were mischievous and <u>slovenly</u>.
    a. neglected
    b. tired
    c. untidy

13. The family had nothing left after their house burned down; they were <u>destitute</u>.
    a. unhappy
    b. impoverished
    c. unprepared

14. I'm <u>famished</u> because I haven't eaten all day.
    a. desperate
    b. sick
    c. very hungry

Name ______________________________

Crossword Puzzle

sincere (113)	horizon (113)	placid (116)	intruders (118)
salvage (124)	threshold (126)	recuperate (126)	edible (128)
infested (128)	crockery (133)	relent (142)	

Directions: Create a crossword puzzle answer key by filling in the grid below. Be sure to number the squares for each word. Blacken any spaces not used by the letters. Then, write clues to the crossword puzzle. Number the clues to match the numbers in the squares. The teacher will give each student a blank grid. Make a blank copy of your crossword puzzle for other students to answer. Exchange your clues with someone else and solve the blank puzzle s/he gives you. Check the completed puzzles with the answer keys.

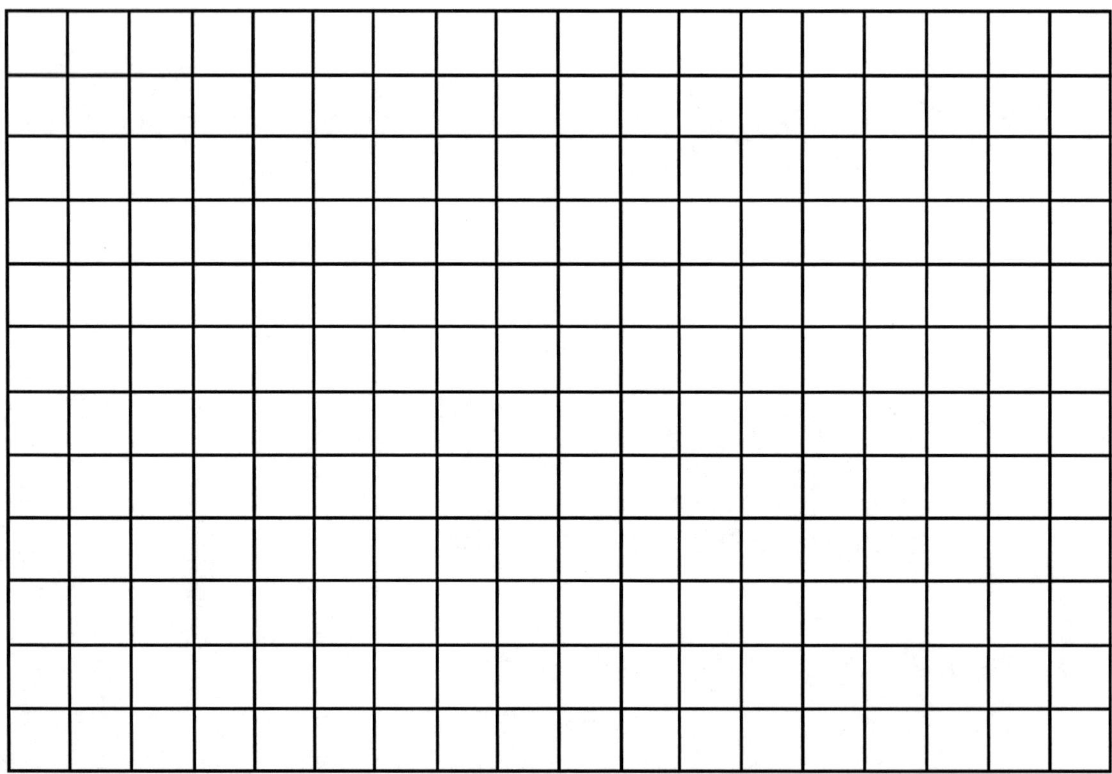

Name ______________________________

Vocabulary Mobile

cobblestones (150)	casket (152)	queasy (155)	tethered (156)
exorbitant (158)	thrive (158)	spineless (161)	cowered (161)
taunts (164)	wraith (166)	apothecary (167)	

Directions: Cut a nine-inch square out of white construction paper. Fold paper in half diagonally (from corner to corner). Unfold paper. Fold the paper in half again (Figure A). Then cut one fold from the outer corner to the center of the paper (Figure B). Slide one cut piece on top of the other to form a triangular shape with a base and two standing sides. Glue the pieces together (Figure C). On the inside base, write a vocabulary word. On the inside left, write a sentence using the vocabulary word. On the inside right, draw a picture to illustrate the vocabulary word. Repeat the process for at least nine words from the list. Glue the back sides of your completed triangles together and hang them as a mobile.

Figure A

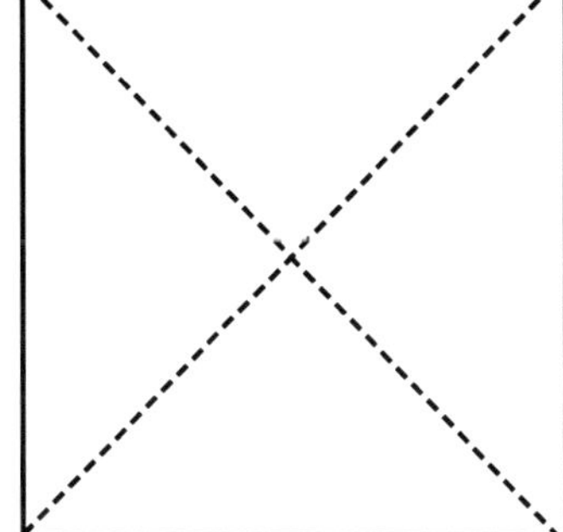

1–Fold in half diagonally

2–Fold in half again

Figure B

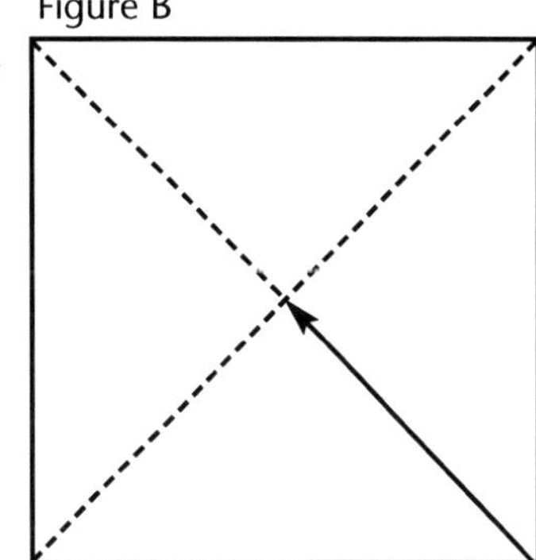

Cut from corner to center in direction of arrow

Figure C

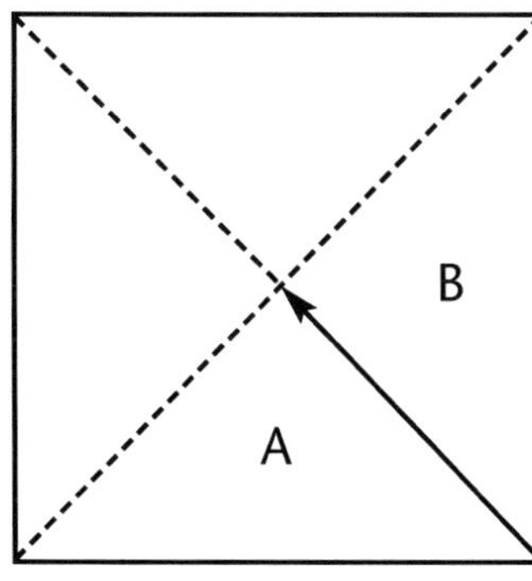

1–Slide one cut piece (A) on top of the other cut piece (B)
2–Glue together to form a triangular shape

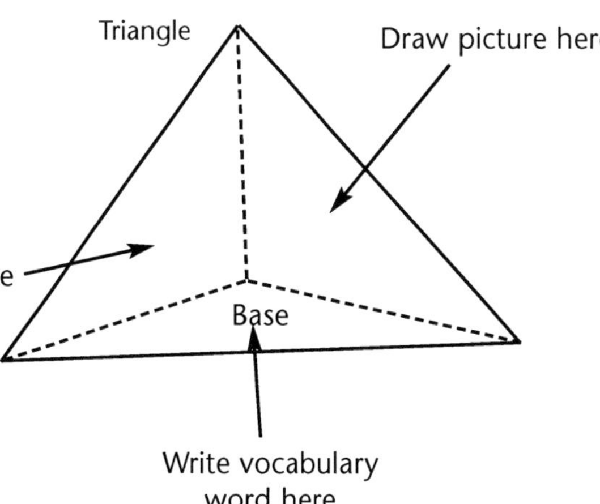

Name ______________________________

Vocabulary Card Game

Teacher Directions:

- Photocopy and cut out the following pages.
- Give one card to each student in the class.
- The student who has the starred card begins by reading his/her question.
- The student who has the card with the correct vocabulary word responds and then reads his/her question.
- Play continues in this manner until all cards have been read.

☆ **cackled**	**enchanted**
Who has a word that means delighted?	Who has a word that means very tired?

weary	**racket**
Who has a word that means loud, distressing noise?	Who has a word that means not allowed?

prohibited	**stoke**
Who has a word that means stir up?	Who has a word that means shriveled or shrunken?

Name ______________________________

withered

Who has a word that means remove?

purge

Who has a word that means threatening?

ominous

Who has a word that means physically weak?

frail

Who has a word that means drive away?

banish

Who has a word that means laughed or talked shrilly?

Name ______________________________

Vocabulary Chart

hovered (210)	vigilant (215)	lingered (215)	swarmed (219)
feign (220)	convey (226)	scoundrel (229)	dashed (234)
begrudge (242)			

Directions: Write each vocabulary word in the left-hand column of the chart. Complete the chart by placing a check mark in the column that best describes your familiarity with each word. Working with a partner, find and read the line where each word appears in the story. Find the meaning of each word in the dictionary. On a separate sheet of paper, use each of the words in the last column in a sentence.

Vocabulary Word	I Can Define	I Have Seen/Heard	New Word For Me

Name ______________________________

Chapters One–Four, pp. 1–23

1. In what city does *Fever 1793* take place?
2. What type of business does the Cook family own?
3. How was Eliza freed from slavery?
4. Who does Mattie consider her best friend?
5. What news does Mrs. Cook bring when she returns from looking for Polly?
6. Why doesn't Mattie's mother want her to go to Polly's house?
7. Name the two pets in the Cook household.
8. What was Grandfather's profession as a young man?

Chapters Five–Seven, pp. 24–53

1. Why does Mattie say that her stomach "flipped over like an egg in a skillet" (p. 30)?
2. What is Mr. Peale's profession?
3. Why does the bell at Christ Church ring so often?
4. What does Mrs. Cook think of Mattie's and Grandfather's dreams for the coffeehouse?
5. Who invites Mattie and her mother to tea?
6. Why does Mrs. Cook insist that Mattie accept the invitation?
7. Why are people suddenly leaving Philadelphia?
8. What is wrong with Colette Ogilvie?

Chapters Eight–Ten, pp. 54–77

1. Who is Andrew Brown?
2. Why doesn't Grandfather think his family should leave Philadelphia?
3. Who is dumped from a wheelbarrow in front of the coffeehouse?
4. Why isn't Mr. Rowley qualified to diagnose Mrs. Cook's illness?
5. Why does Mattie's mother beg Mattie to stop taking care of her?
6. After Dr. Kerr diagnoses Mother with yellow fever, what does he recommend they do with Mattie?
7. Who sends Mattie flowers?

Name ______________________________

Chapters Eleven–Fifteen, pp. 78–112

1. Why do the soldiers stop the wagon on its way to Pembroke?
2. When the soldiers agree to let the farmer and his wife pass through, what does the farmer do to Mattie and Grandfather?
3. Why is Mattie anxious to find a willow tree?
4. How does Mattie plan to catch a fish without a fishing rod?
5. After Mattie collapses, where does Grandfather take her?
6. Who is Mrs. Flagg?
7. What do the doctors at Bush Hill think of bleeding people to cure them of a fever?
8. Once Mattie recovers, where do she and Grandfather plan to go?

Chapters Sixteen–Nineteen, pp. 113–149

1. Why does Mrs. Bowles want Mattie to come to the orphanage?
2. How does Philadelphia look when Mattie and Grandfather arrive?
3. Is the coffeehouse just as the family left it?
4. What does Mattie find for Grandfather and herself to eat?
5. How often did Mattie normally bathe before the epidemic?
6. Why does Mattie decide to sleep downstairs?
7. What awakens Mattie in the night?
8. How does Grandfather die?

Chapters Twenty–Twenty-two, pp. 150–177

1. How does Mattie dignify her grandfather's burial?
2. Why does Mattie go to see Andrew Brown?
3. What does Mattie find in a doorway on her way back to the coffeehouse?
4. What is Eliza doing when Mattie spots her on the streets?
5. What does Eliza tell Mattie about her mother?
6. Who lives with Eliza?
7. Why did Dr. Benjamin Rush ask the Free African Society to help take care of the sick?

Name ______________________________

Chapters Twenty-three–Twenty-five, pp. 178–208

1. What does Mother Smith try to convince Mattie to do with Nell?
2. Why couldn't Colette Ogilvie marry the man her mother wanted her to marry?
3. Where do Joseph and Eliza decide Mattie should live as long as there is disease in Philadelphia?
4. Who goes with Eliza to visit and take care of the sick?
5. What happens to Joseph's sons?
6. Where do Mattie and Eliza decide to take the sick children?
7. Why doesn't Mattie want Eliza to bleed the children?

Chapters Twenty-six–Epilogue, pp. 209–243

1. When Mattie awakens in the garden, what does she see?
2. How does food become available again?
3. What does Mattie learn when she asks about her mother in town?
4. What did the Peale household eat during the epidemic?
5. How does Nathaniel and Mattie's relationship change?
6. Who does Mattie announce as her partner at the coffeehouse?
7. Why is there a parade down High Street?
8. What is Mrs. Cook's condition when she finally returns to the coffeehouse?
9. How does the book "start over" at the end?

Name ______________________________

Concept Map

Directions: Complete the Concept Map below.

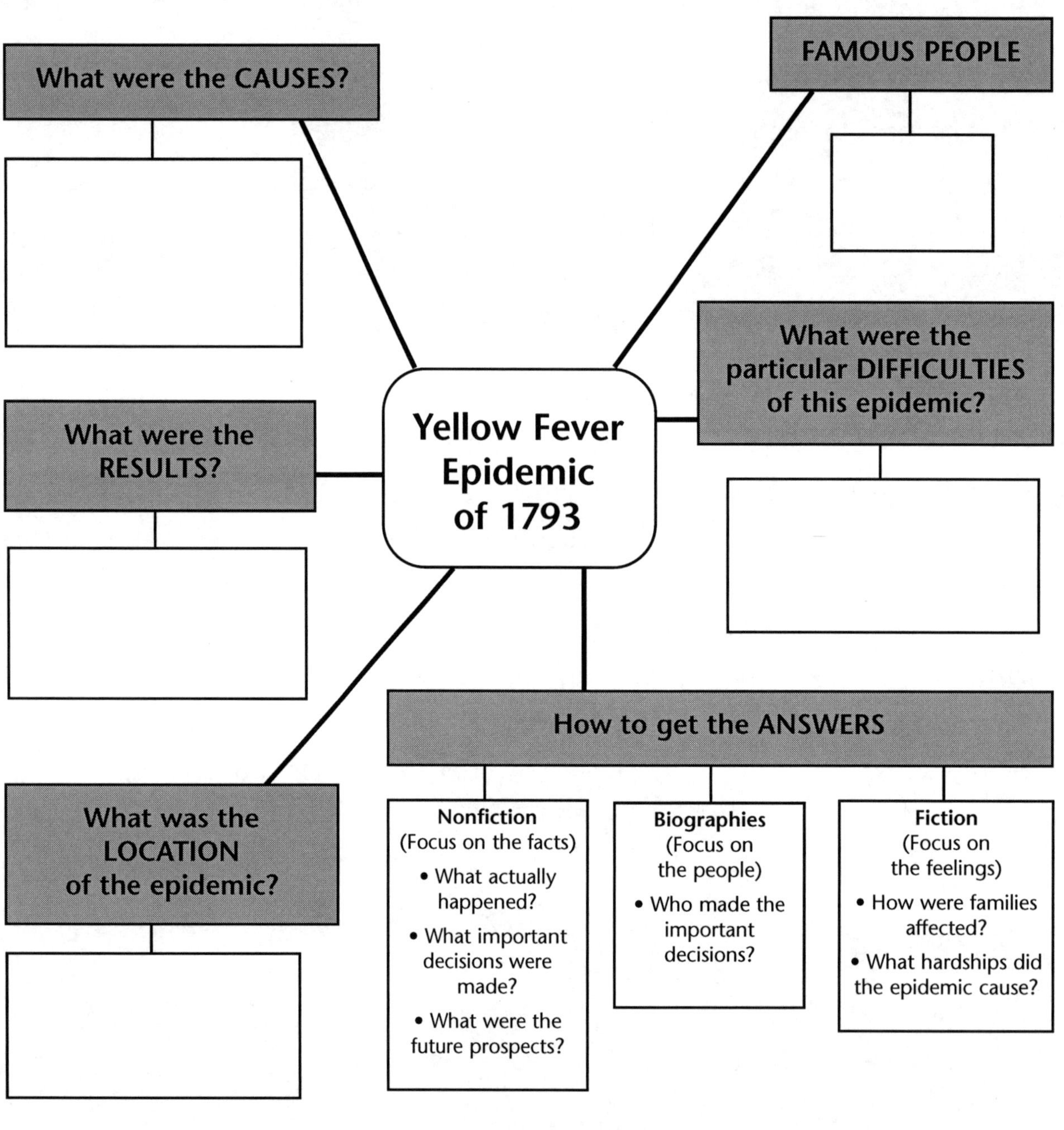

Name ______________________________

Story Map

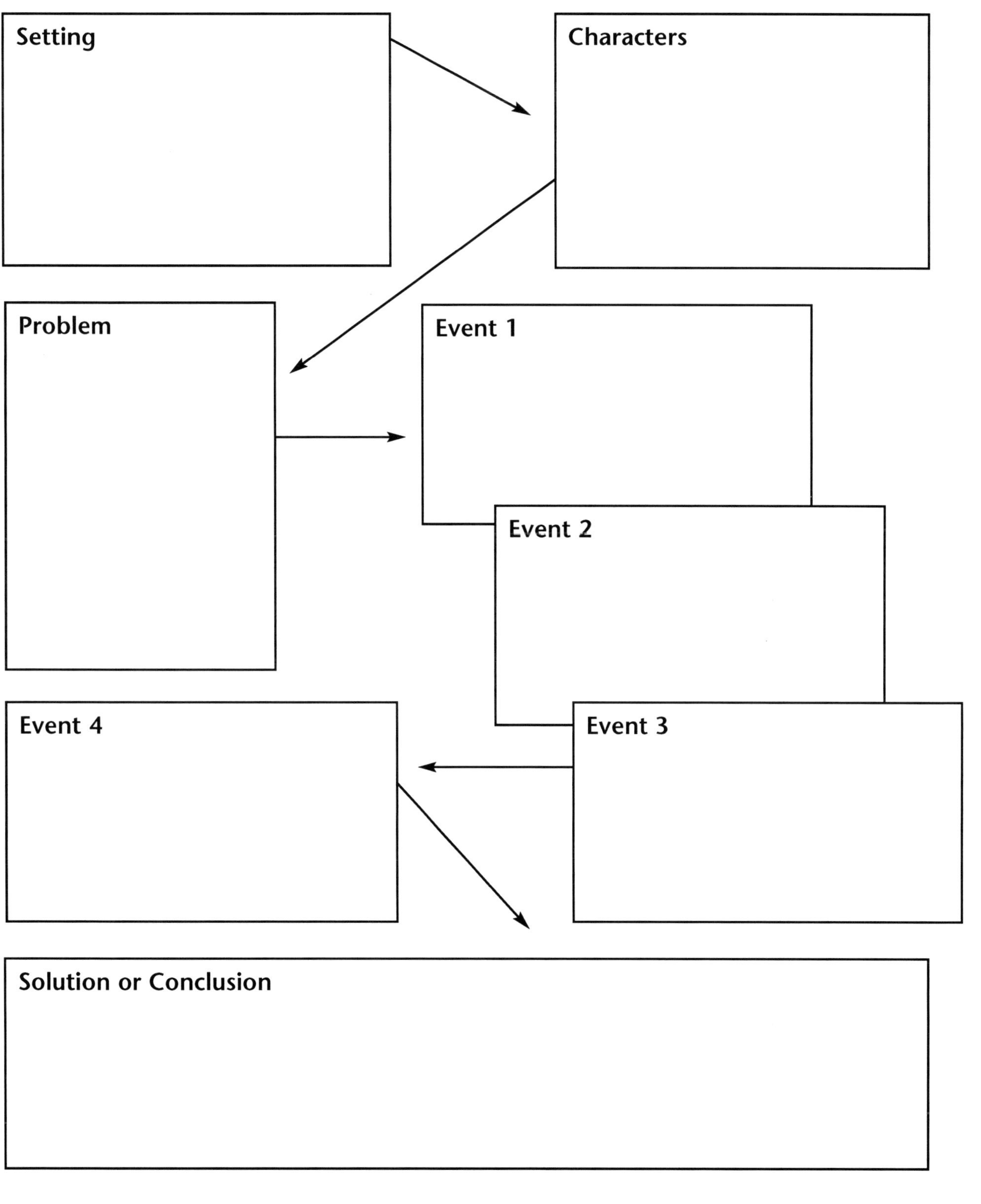

Name ______________________________

Character Analysis Blocks

Directions: Select a character from the book to describe using the blocks below.

	Who is the character?		
	What does the character do?	*Why does s/he do it?*	
What, if anything, is significant about the character's name?	*What is the nature of this character's actions? (reactive, active, important, consequential, secondary)*	*What is the significance of the book's time and place to the character?*	
What is unusual or important about the character?	*How does the character change in the story?*	*Does the character remind you of another character from another book? Who?*	*Do you know anyone similar to this character?*

Name ______________________________

Character Chart

Directions: In the boxes across from each of the feelings, describe an incident or time in the book when each of the listed characters experienced that feeling. You may use "not applicable" if you cannot find an example.

	Mattie	Mrs. Cook	Grandfather	Eliza
Frustration				
Anger				
Fear				
Humiliation				
Relief				
Triumph				

Name ______________________________

Cause/Effect Chart

Directions: Make a flow chart to show decisions a character made, the decisions s/he could have made, and the result(s) of each. (Use your imagination to speculate on the results of decisions the character could have made.)

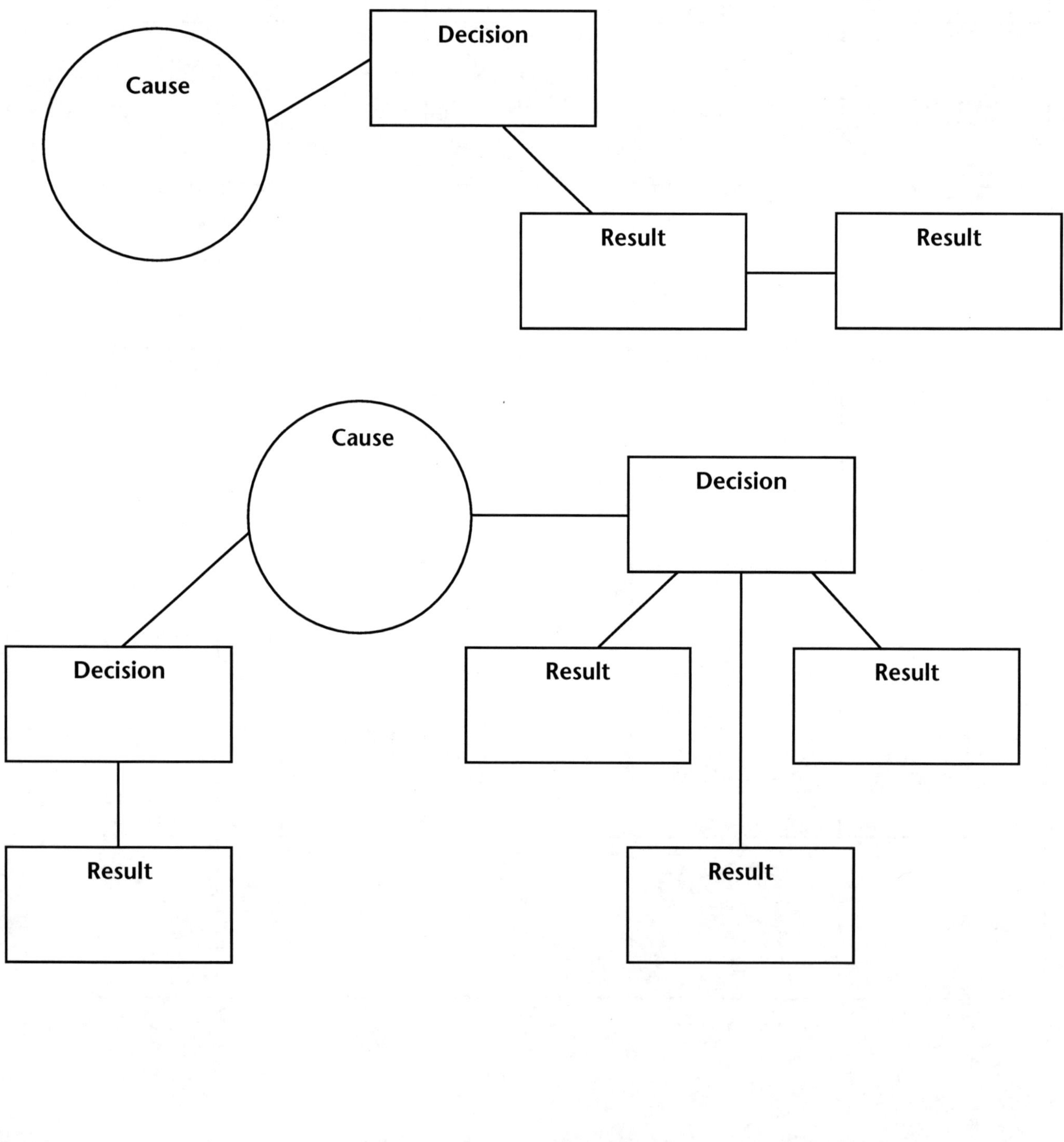

Name ______________________________

I'm A Star!

Directions: A movie is being made of *Fever 1793*, and you are chosen to be one of the stars of the movie. Describe in detail the character you want to be and explain why you chose this character.

Name ______________________________

Directions: Write an article about the panic caused by the yellow fever epidemic.

The Daily News

Name ______________________________

Fever 1793
Quiz #1
Chapters One–Seven, pp. 1–53

A. Multiple Choice: Choose the BEST answer.

1. What is the Cook family business?
   a. farming
   b. coffeehouse
   c. pharmacy
   d. blacksmith

2. What happened to Mattie's father?
   a. He died during the war.
   b. He was killed in a farming accident.
   c. He died of pneumonia.
   d. He fell off a ladder and broke his neck.

3. Who is the coffeehouse serving girl?
   a. Polly
   b. Eliza
   c. Mattie
   d. Silas

4. Why does Mattie's mother refuse to allow her to visit Polly's family?
   a. Polly's family lives in a dangerous part of town.
   b. Mother is afraid Mattie could catch whatever illness Polly had.
   c. Mother needs Mattie at the coffeehouse to work.
   d. Mother doesn't want Mattie going out in the dark.

5. What was Grandfather's profession?
   a. doctor
   b. coffeehouse owner
   c. army officer
   d. farmer

Name ______________________________

B. Short Answer

1. Where does Mattie go to get new supplies of food for the coffeehouse?

2. What is Nathaniel Benson studying?

3. How does Mrs. Cook feel about Grandfather's and Mattie's dreams for the coffeehouse?

4. What special invitation do Mrs. Cook and Mattie receive?

5. What happens to Colette Ogilvie?

C. True/False

___ 1. Mattie is excited about Mother's suggestion that she stay with the Ludingtons in the country.

___ 2. The Eplers sell chickens and eggs at the market.

___ 3. Mother has hopes of Mattie marrying Nathaniel Benson.

___ 4. When a person dies of yellow fever, the church bell rings once for every year he/she lived.

___ 5. The Ogilvies make Mattie feel comfortable and welcome in their home.

Name ______________________________

Fever 1793
Quiz #2
Chapters Eight–Fifteen, pp. 54–112

A. Short Answer

1. What did many of Philadelphia's wealthy families do to avoid getting sick?

2. How does Grandfather respond to the talk of an epidemic in Philadelphia?

3. When mother falls ill while running errands, how is she brought home?

4. Is Mr. Rowley qualified to diagnose Mother's illness? Why or why not?

5. Why doesn't Mother want Mattie to take care of her?

6. How is Dr. Kerr's diagnosis of Mother's illness different from Mr. Rowley's?

7. What does Dr. Kerr recommend the family do with Matilda?

8. Who will stay with Mattie? Who will stay with Mother?

9. What does Nathaniel send Mattie?

B. Multiple Choice: Choose the BEST answer.

1. Why do the soldiers stop the farmer's wagon on the road to Gwynedd?
   a. They want to rob the farmer.
   b. They want to warn them of danger ahead.
   c. They want to stop any sick people from entering the town.
   d. They want to inspect the wagon for weapons.

Name ______________________________

2. What does the farmer do with Mattie and Grandfather?
   a. He leaves them on the side of the road.
   b. He takes them back to Philadelphia.
   c. He leaves them with the soldiers.
   d. He takes them to a home for the sick.

3. Why does Grandfather tell Mattie he's a "fool"?
   a. because he is too old to take care of Mattie
   b. because he shouldn't have gotten sick
   c. because he should have taken the epidemic in Philadelphia more seriously
   d. because he shouldn't have taken Mattie away from home

4. How does Mattie try to catch fish?
   a. She makes a pole from a tree branch.
   b. She uses her skirt as a net.
   c. She uses her bonnet as a net.
   d. She uses a blanket to trap the fish.

5. When Mattie gets yellow fever, where does Grandfather take her?
   a. Bush Hill
   b. the Ludingtons
   c. home to Philadelphia
   d. a farmer's house

6. How is the treatment of yellow fever different at Bush Hill?
   a. They give everyone a private room.
   b. They do not believe in bleeding patients.
   c. There are no doctors, just nurses like Mrs. Flagg.
   d. They shut all the windows to keep mosquitoes out.

7. While Mattie is recovering, what does Grandfather do?
   a. He rests, trying to regain his strength.
   b. He leaves Mattie and goes back to Philadelphia.
   c. He goes to the Ludingtons to try to find Mrs. Cook.
   d. He helps the doctors and nurses at Bush Hill.

8. When Mattie recovers, what does Grandfather decide they should do?
   a. He decides Mattie should go to the orphanage while he searches for Mrs. Cook.
   b. He decides Mattie should stay at Bush Hill and help take care of patients.
   c. He decides they should return to the coffeehouse.
   d. He decides they should go to the Ludingtons.

Name ______________________________

A. True/False

___ 1. Mattie tells Mrs. Bowles she will work at the orphanage.

___ 2. Grandfather and Mattie discover the coffeehouse just as they left it.

___ 3. Mattie can barely find enough food in the garden to make dinner.

___ 4. Mattie carries water from the river for her bath.

___ 5. Mattie sleeps downstairs because it is cooler than her bedroom.

B. Short Answer

1. What is the sound that awakens Mattie in the night?

2. What happens to Grandfather when he tries to protect Mattie?

3. What does Mattie use to chase the robbers away?

4. How does the struggle with the robbers end?

5. What does Mattie insist be done at Grandfather's funeral?

C. Multiple Choice: Choose the BEST answer.

1. Why does Grandfather's funeral feel wrong to Mattie?
   a. It is not the funeral she feels such a great man deserves.
   b. She wishes her mother and all of his friends could be there.
   c. She wishes there were a loud and long funeral procession.
   d. All of the above.

Name ______________________________

2. Why does Andrew Brown stay in Philadelphia?
   a. He doesn't have anywhere to go.
   b. He doesn't believe there is an epidemic.
   c. The newspaper is the only means of communication in the city.
   d. He loves his work too much to quit.

3. Who does Mattie find alone in the corner of a house?
   a. Nell
   b. Eliza
   c. Mrs. Cook
   d. Nathaniel

4. What is Eliza doing when Mattie spots her on the street?
   a. returning from the market
   b. visiting the sick
   c. going to church
   d. playing with her nephews

5. Where is Eliza living?
   a. the coffeehouse
   b. the Free African Society home
   c. her brother Joseph's home
   d. in the church basement

6. Why is Joseph so sad?
   a. His wife died.
   b. One of his children died.
   c. He has lost his job and cannot support his family.
   d. His wife is missing.

7. Who is Mother Smith?
   a. the manager of the Free African Society
   b. Joseph's mother
   c. Nell's grandmother
   d. the caretaker of Joseph's home and his children

8. Why did Dr. Rush ask members of the Free African Society to help take care of the sick?
   a. He believed black people could not catch the fever.
   b. He didn't care if black people got sick.
   c. He thought they were well-organized and would be good helpers.
   d. Reverend Allen owed him a favor.

Name ______________________________

Fever 1793
Quiz #4
Chapters Twenty-three–Epilogue, pp. 178–243

A. Short Answer

1. What does Mother Smith try to convince Mattie to do with Nell?

2. Why does Mattie keep Nell instead of following Mother Smith's advice?

3. What did Colette Ogilvie do that humiliated her family and amused everyone else?

4. What happens when Mattie and Eliza pass the Peale home?

5. What is the hardest thing for Mattie to deal with when she visits the sick with Eliza?

6. What do Mattie and Eliza discover when they return from their visits to the sick?

7. Where do Mattie and Eliza decide to take the sick children?

8. Why does Mattie tell Eliza not to bleed the children?

B. Multiple Choice: Choose the BEST answer.

1. What does Mattie see when she awakens in the garden?
   a. Mother
   b. Nathaniel
   c. frost on the weeds
   d. fruit on the trees

2. What does Joseph send with a messenger?
   a. news of Mother
   b. flowers
   c. food
   d. clothing for the children

Name ______________________________

3. What promise do the Eplers make to Mattie at the market?
   a. to ask everyone if they have seen her mother
   b. to deliver a chicken to the coffeehouse
   c. to come see her at the marketplace the next day
   d. to take Mattie to the country to look for her mother

4. Who becomes a regular visitor at the coffeehouse?
   a. Andrew Brown
   b. Nathaniel Benson
   c. the Eplers
   d. Joseph

5. What is Mattie's plan?
   a. to sell the coffeehouse and use the money for food
   b. to sell the coffeehouse to Joseph and Eliza
   c. to make Eliza her partner at the coffeehouse
   d. to expand the coffeehouse into the empty store next door

6. Why is there a parade down High Street?
   a. The city is honoring all the victims of the yellow fever.
   b. There is a celebration for the end of the epidemic.
   c. George Washington is returning to the city.
   d. The city is welcoming back all the people who fled the city.

7. Who is in a carriage at the end of the parade?
   a. Mrs. Cook
   b. the President's cabinet
   c. the Ogilvies
   d. Dr. Benjamin Rush

8. How does Mother appear to Mattie?
   a. She hasn't changed a bit.
   b. She appears healthy after months in the country.
   c. She looks angry about all the changes to the coffeehouse.
   d. She is weak and frail.

9. How does Mattie feel at the conclusion of the novel?
   a. She is hoping to marry Edward Ogilvie.
   b. She wishes she didn't have so much work to do.
   c. She resents having to take care of her mother.
   d. She is happy and optimistic about the future.

Name ______________________________

A. Ordering: Number these events in the order in which they happened.

____ Mrs. Cook gets yellow fever.
____ The first frost appears.
____ Grandfather dies.
____ Polly dies.
____ Mattie and Grandfather stay at Bush Hill.
____ Mattie goes to the Ogilvies' tea party.
____ Mattie gets yellow fever.
____ Mattie finds Nell.
____ Eliza and Mattie move the sick children to the coffeehouse.
____ Mattie and Nell move in with Eliza.

B. Short Answer

1. In what city and year does the novel take place?

2. Name one way in which medicine in the eighteenth century was different from modern medicine.

3. Describe an incident or character in the novel that you found to be funny.

4. What surprised you most about the descriptions of life in the eighteenth century?

5. Why don't we see yellow fever epidemics in the United States anymore?

C. Essay: Choose one of the following and write a well-developed essay of at least three paragraphs.

1. How does Mattie change throughout the novel? Explain what you think causes these changes.
2. Do you appreciate anything more in your own life after reading *Fever 1793*? If so, what is it and why?
3. Apply one of the major themes of the novel to your own life.

Answer Key

Activity #1: Dedication: "This book is for my father, Reverend Frank A. Halse, Jr., the finest man I know."; Title: *Fever 1793*; Cover Illustration: the face of a girl with yellow eyes; Teasers on the cover: the girl's yellow eyes, "The plot rages like the epidemic itself." (The *New York Times* Book Review); Friends' Recommendations: Answers will vary; Reviewers' recommendations/awards won: ALA Best Book for Young Adults, Junior Library Guild Selection, "A gripping story..."; Predictions: Answers will vary.

Activity #2: 1. h 2. c 3. b 4. a 5. g 6. f 7. d 8. e

Activities #3–#5: Answers will vary.

Activity #6: 1. a 2. b 3. b 4. a 5. b 6. b 7. c 8. a 9. b 10. a 11. b 12. c 13. b 14. c

Activities #7–#8: Answers will vary.

Activity #9: Students will play the Vocabulary Card Game.

Activity #10: Answers will vary.

Study Guide

Chapters One–Four: 1. Philadelphia (p. 4) 2. a coffeehouse (p. 7) 3. Her husband bought her freedom (pp. 8–9). 4. Eliza (p. 9) 5. Polly, the coffeehouse serving girl, is dead (p. 13). 6. She's afraid Mattie will catch an illness (p. 16). 7. Silas the cat and King George the parrot (pp. 3, 18) 8. army officer (p. 19)

Chapters Five–Seven: 1. She sees Nathaniel Benson (p. 30). 2. artist (p. 30) 3. It rings every time someone dies (p. 32). 4. She thinks they are foolish (pp. 37–39). 5. Pernilla Ogilvie (p. 41) 6. She hopes Mattie will marry Edward Ogilvie (p. 43). 7. They're afraid of catching yellow fever (p. 50). 8. She has yellow fever (p. 53).

Chapters Eight–Ten: 1. newspaper editor (p. 57) 2. He doesn't believe there is an epidemic (pp. 59–60). 3. Mrs. Cook (p. 62) 4. He isn't a real doctor, just a local "quack" (pp. 64–65). 5. She knows she might be contagious, and she doesn't want Mattie to get sick (p. 69). 6. take her out of the city (p. 73) 7. Nathaniel Benson (p. 75)

Chapters Eleven–Fifteen: 1. They want to check all travelers for yellow fever to keep the disease from spreading (p. 81). 2. He leaves Mattie and Grandfather on the side of the road (p. 83). 3. She believes if she finds willow trees, she will find water (p. 85). 4. by using her skirt as a net (pp. 90–91) 5. a hospital at Bush Hill (p. 101) 6. the nurse who cares for Mattie and Grandfather (p. 99) 7. They don't think it works (p. 103). 8. home to Philadelphia (p. 112)

Chapters Sixteen–Nineteen: 1. to work (p. 115) 2. It is in chaos. Dead people are lying everywhere, and the air is filled with the stench of death (pp. 118–120). 3. No, someone has broken in and ransacked it (pp. 122–124). 4. small, rotten vegetables from the garden (p. 128) 5. once a month (p. 131) 6. She can't sleep with Grandfather snoring (p. 136). 7. footsteps (p. 138) 8. He is injured during the fight with the robbers (pp. 144–147).

Chapters Twenty–Twenty-two: 1. She insists on a prayer and reads from the Bible (pp. 153–154). 2. She wants to place an ad to see if anyone has seen her mother (p. 157). 3. an orphaned girl named Nell (p. 161) 4. visiting the sick (p. 167) 5. She went to the country to find Mattie and Grandfather (p. 171). 6. Eliza's brother, Joseph, and his sons, Robert and William (p. 171) 7. He thought African Americans couldn't catch yellow fever (pp. 175–176).

Chapters Twenty-three–Twenty-five: 1. take her to the orphanage (p. 180) 2. She had already married her French tutor (p. 186). 3. with them (p. 189) 4. Mattie (pp. 192–196) 5. They get yellow fever (p. 197). 6. to the coffeehouse (p. 199) 7. She knows it doesn't work, and she's afraid it killed her mother (pp. 205–206).

Chapters Twenty-six–Epilogue: 1. frost (pp. 209–210) 2. The farmers have come back to the market (p. 211). 3. nothing (p. 214) 4. specimens from Mr. Peale's natural history museum (p. 217) 5. They see each other all the time, and they are no longer awkward around each other (throughout). 6. Eliza (p. 224) 7. George Washington has returned to town (p. 231). 8. She is weak and frail (pp. 234–235). 9. Mattie is waking up, and Silas is chasing a mouse (p. 240).

Note: Answers to Activities #11–#17 will vary, but suggested answers are given where applicable.

Activity #11: Answers will vary

Activity #12: Setting: Philadelphia, 1793; Characters: Matilda, Mrs. Cook, Eliza, Nathaniel, Grandfather, Nell, Joseph, Mrs. Flagg; Problem: There is a yellow fever epidemic in Philadelphia.; Event 1: Polly dies.; Event 2: Mrs. Cook gets yellow fever, and Grandfather takes Mattie to the country.; Event 3: Mattie and Grandfather survive yellow fever and return to find Philadelphia in chaos.; Event 4: Mattie finds Eliza after Grandfather dies, and they help each other survive.; Solution or Conclusion: Frost kills the disease-carrying mosquitoes, Mattie and Eliza enter into a partnership at the coffeehouse, and Mrs. Cook returns.

Activity #13: Mrs. Cook; owns a coffeehouse; husband died, leaving her to support family; N/A; harsh, no-nonsense; unusual for a woman to be in charge of business then; despite her strength, gets yellow fever and disappears; after surviving yellow fever, is much more gentle and loving toward people; Answers will vary; Answers will vary.

Activity #14: Character—Matilda; Frustration—Her mother makes her go to the Ogilvies' home for tea so they can get information about Edward Ogilvie.; Anger—People broke into the coffeehouse and left it in shambles.; Fear—Grandfather has died, her mother is missing, and she is hungry and alone.; Humiliation—most of the time when she's talking to Nathaniel Benson; Relief—She finds Eliza after searching for someone familiar.; Triumph—She survives yellow fever and opens the coffeehouse again.

Activity #15: Cause—Yellow fever has infected the Cook home.; Decision—Grandfather is to take Mattie to the country to keep her safe.; Result—Everyone is gone, so the house is broken into and the food is stolen.; Result—Grandfather and Mattie are abandoned when Grandfather becomes ill.; Result—Grandfather and Mattie return home, but they have no food and are targets for robbers.; Decision he/she could have made—Mattie could have stayed somewhere in the city so that she and Grandfather would not have been left on the side of the road and the house would not have been robbed.

Activities #16–#17: Answers will vary.

Quiz #1: **A.** 1. b (p. 7) 2. d (p. 7) 3. a (p. 10) 4. b (p. 16) 5. c (p. 19) **B.** 1. the market (p. 27) 2. art (p. 30) 3. She thinks they are foolish (pp. 37–39). 4. Pernilla Ogilvie has invited them to tea (p. 41). 5. She becomes ill with yellow fever and collapses (p. 53). **C.** 1. F (pp. 25–26) 2. T (p. 28) 3. F (p. 30) 4. T (p. 32) 5. F (pp. 48–53)

Quiz #2: **A.** 1. They fled the city (p. 54). 2. He refuses to believe there's an epidemic (pp. 57–60). 3. in a wheelbarrow (pp. 61–62) 4. No, he's not a real doctor (p. 64). 5. She doesn't want her to get sick (p. 69). 6. Dr. Kerr says Mother has yellow fever (p. 71). 7. send her to the country (p. 73) 8. Grandfather; Eliza (p. 74) 9. a painting of flowers (p. 75) **B.** 1. c (p. 81) 2. a (p. 83) 3. c (p. 87) 4. b (pp. 90–91) 5. a (p. 101) 6. b (p. 103) 7. d (p. 108) 8. c (pp. 111–112)

Quiz #3: **A.** 1. F (pp. 115–116) 2. F (pp. 122–124) 3. T (pp. 127–128) 4. F (p. 131) 5. F (p. 136) **B.** 1. footsteps (p. 138) 2. One of the robbers kills him (p. 145). 3. Grandfather's sword (p. 146) 4. Grandfather dies. Mattie prepares his body for burial (pp. 146–149). 5. a prayer be said (pp. 153–154) **C.** 1. d (pp. 152–154) 2. c (p. 157) 3. a (p. 161) 4. b (p. 167) 5. c (pp. 170–171) 6. a (p. 171) 7. d (pp. 172–173) 8. a (pp. 175–176)

Quiz #4: **A.** 1. take her to the orphanage (p. 180) 2. She can't bear to leave her at the overcrowded orphanage (pp. 184–185). 3. She married her French tutor (p. 186). 4. Nathaniel throws flowers to her (p. 188). 5. the heartache (p. 192) 6. The children are sick with yellow fever (pp. 197–198). 7. the coffeehouse (p. 199) 8. She learned at Bush Hill that bleeding only causes people to get worse (pp. 205–206). **B.** 1. c (pp. 209–210) 2. c (p. 211) 3. a (p. 214) 4. b (p. 219) 5. c (p. 224) 6. c (p. 231) 7. a (p. 233) 8. d (pp. 234–239) 9. d (pp. 242–243)

Novel Test: **A.** (from top to bottom) 3, 10, 6, 1, 5, 2, 4, 7, 9, 8 **B.** 1. Philadelphia; 1793 2. Answers will vary. Suggestions: bleeding patients, treating with herbs, lack of understanding of how diseases spread 3. Answers will vary. 4. Answers will vary. Suggestions: the clothing, people didn't bathe often 5. We understand the disease and how it's spread; we inspect ships that enter U.S. harbors for disease; we have better sanitation and sewage treatment. **C.** Refer to the scoring rubric on page 36 of this guide.

Linking Novel Units® Student Packets to National and State Reading Assessments

During the past several years, an increasing number of students have faced some form of state-mandated competency testing in reading. Many states now administer state-developed assessments to measure the skills and knowledge emphasized in their particular reading curriculum. This Novel Units® guide includes open-ended comprehension questions that correlate with state-mandated reading assessments. The rubric below provides important information for evaluating responses to open-ended comprehension questions. Teachers may also use scoring rubrics provided for their own state's competency test.

Scoring Rubric for Open-Ended Items

3-Exemplary	Thorough, complete ideas/information Clear organization throughout Logical reasoning/conclusions Thorough understanding of reading task Accurate, complete response
2-Sufficient	Many relevant ideas/pieces of information Clear organization throughout most of response Minor problems in logical reasoning/conclusions General understanding of reading task Generally accurate and complete response
1-Partially Sufficient	Minimally relevant ideas/information Obvious gaps in organization Obvious problems in logical reasoning/conclusions Minimal understanding of reading task Inaccuracies/incomplete response
0-Insufficient	Irrelevant ideas/information No coherent organization Major problems in logical reasoning/conclusions Little or no understanding of reading task Generally inaccurate/incomplete response